CACTI

Huberta von Bronsart

revised by Walter Luthi

Haynes

**explains
series**

A BOOK IN THE Haynes EXPLAINS SERIES

CACTI is published
by
The Haynes Publishing Group of Sparkford, Yeovil, Somerset, BA22 7JJ,
England
First published in German under the title
KAKTEEN
by
Hallwag AG of Bern, Switzerland

© English language edition, The Haynes Publishing Group 1977
First published July 1977

ISBN 0 85429 523 2

English language translation "Translance" of Manchester
Printed and bound in Great Britain
Cover photograph Franz Rychener (Echinocereus acifer Lem.)
Photographs Heinrich Hofmanner, Walter Luthi and Franz Rychener
Classification Hans Krainz

CONTENTS

What are Cacti?

Cacti are the strangest creatures we meet in the plant kingdom. They are green like other plants but they stand on their own as succulent, ribbed stem, warty globular shapes, and some of them twist themselves snakelike around a support; they have no leaves, only spines (often wrongly called thorns); sometimes these spines are in bristly bundles, sometimes they are threatening, sharp and spiky, sometimes they are paper-thin and flat; there are some species which are enveloped in silvery white, silky, downwards hanging hair. In short, cacti are unique.

However, in the fullness of time, a spiny dwarf can grow a bud which breaks forth into a flower of indescribable beauty of form and unexpected brightness of colour: a wholly improbable but wonderful flower. Comical looking, small balls of spines decorate themselves with a wreath of bright red, white, yellow or pink flowers. On *Nyctocereus grandiflorus,* half a dozen or as many as a dozen, large white scented flowers will open one night, but by early morning this luxuriance hangs down, wilted and unattractive; however, even the glory of these few hours is sufficient to call this plant 'The Queen of the Night' and to lavish loving care upon it.

A joy of this kind is given by cacti to those who handle them correctly. Frequently, however, we hear hard words about cacti: they are boring, lovably misshapen plant dwarfs, which do not display any bright, green growth. At one time, when they were given as presents, they flowered very beautifully, but now they stand, unhappy and dusty looking, in some corner of the room; they do not grow any buds; only small grey bugs lurk between the ribs or the warts. Really, their skin is beginning to shrivel up — away with them into the dustbin!

Cacti behave in this manner only if they fall into the wrong hands, and meet people who think that they are desert plants which do not require any water and can be left quietly for several days or weeks unwatered and that they are plants which require no everyday care.

Nevertheless, cacti are not wholly foolproof. They are certainly adapted to drought conditions but, strange as it may seem, they must be watered and they may even be provided with fertiliser just like other plants. Growing of cacti is not difficult, but they require care, like any living being which one intends to thrive. As 'drought resistant plants', they are adapted to consume water sparingly: they have their 'evaporating surfaces' which are limited to an extreme degree by not having leaves. Only the *genus Pereskia* (which is difficult for amateurs to grow) has genuine leaves; all the others have transformed these into spines, which, in the majority of cases, are arranged into cushion like structures (areoles) which often carry small yellowish brown hairy tufts known as glochids.

The leaves, however, are most important feeding organs: the carbon dioxide in the air is processed by the chlorophyll in the leaf cells, into starch and plant building materials. In cacti, this assimilation process in the leaves is replaced by the assimilating surface of the whole plant whose surface cells contain chlorophyll. These plants increase this surface area by providing the globular and stem shaped forms with tubercles or longitudinal ribs; the *Epiphyllum Opuntia* and *Zygocactus* have stems of segments which are flattened in leaf form.

Cacti belong to the group of plants known as 'succulents'. Their stems store water in cells containing glutinous matter in order to have this water available in times of drought. These plants are never quite without water even in the desert, because a heavy dew falls during the clear nights and the cacti can absorb this moisture with their fine roots which are spread out close to the ground surface. Added to this is the fact that in areas where cacti grow, there will always be a rainy period, however short, once a year which will richly provide the cacti with water for storing. It is quite wrong to think that cacti will not suffer if they are not watered for days, because no dew will fall on the flower pots on the window sill!

The *Zygocactus* and the *Epiphyllum* are epiphytes, ie. they do not live on the ground, but in the leaf mould which is collected into the base of forks, of tree branches in tropical jungles. Their home is in the jungles of Brazil or Mexico, Central and South America. In North America, the vegetation zone of the wintering opuntias reaches as far as Arizona. Hence they have a certain amount of moisture available all the year round and they are hardly ever exposed to direct light. This fact must be considered in the cultivation of these cacti; they need humus-rich soil, more moisture than other cacti and they must never be exposed to direct sunlight.

There are cacti which grow in deserts, wastelands and mountains, and they all must be considered differently from the cultivation point of view, depending on the conditions of their original home.

Shelter and general care

The ideal position for the collection of cacti is a small, heated greenhouse in the garden; however, not many gardeners can afford this. A grower who cultivates only a few cacti obviously places them between other pot plants in the window. A warm glass box is recommended for a collection of smaller cacti, for seedlings and for somewhat more sensitive species which must be protected against dust; this box is placed in a suitable position in the open from early spring to late autumn. This box can be built from timber, or better still, with light alloy open structure, in which case the members which support the glazing can be narrower. The side walls can also be made from glass: light must be available unimpeded from all sides. The smaller such a box is, the more fiercely the air in it is heated by the sun. This heat can become excessive for cacti: they will suffer sunburn or they will dry out. It must also be ensured that the box is generously aired. In the box the plants are planted in trays or placed into trays which are filled with peat moss. This seating into peat moss is not necessary if plastic pots are used.

Generally speaking, cacti are handled in the same way as other pot plants: they must be placed in a good light and in circulating air but they must be protected against draughts. They all require a resting period if they are expected to flower: they must then be kept at a lower temperature (but still in good light) and watered sparingly. With the exception of the *Zygocactus,* this resting period is usually in the wintertime; during this period the majority of plants find a temperature of 6—12°C (46—52°F) favourable. The new growing period begins in spring and at this time the plants are sensitive to direct sunlight which they can otherwise bear quite well in the summertime. They must be generously watered during their growth period like other indoor plants; they will also enjoy a fine spray of water especially during the hot summer. The winter flowering plants which would also like to be warm in winter, must also be sprayed during this period. Lukewarm water must always be used for this purpose, never cold tap water.

The majority of cacti are readily accommodated in conventional flower pots; some of the cacti which form long turnip-like roots require tall narrow pots; others, with especially flat roots, are best planted in flat pots or trays.

In all cases the soil must be porous. The usual garden soil is unacceptable for cacti as for other pot plants. Among the large number of recipes for soils for growing cacti the following has generally been found the most useful: good, old leaf mould, friable clay and sharp, lime free sand, mixed in equal parts, with the addition of small pieces of broken brick. Only the epiphytes, ie. *zygocactus* and *epiphyllum* must have soil enriched with humus; for this purpose a proportion of the clay is replaced by well rotted manure. Ready made 'soil for cacti' is available from all good garden centres. Cacti like slightly acid soil, ie. it must have as little lime as possible. A very hard (lime rich) water must be allowed to settle for at least a day before watering so that most of the lime will be precipitated: pure rain water is best for watering. Watering must not be carried out at the temperature of tap water; the water must be allowed to stand until it has reached room temperature.

Nowadays watering is carried out from below. If this is done the hairy plants in particular will be less susceptible to rotting. If the pots or trays have become excessively dry (which can occur, for example, in the winter resting time) then it is useful to immerse them up to their upper edge in water kept at room temperature until the soil surface also has become wet. In this case, the plants themselves remain quite dry which is very important in winter, especially for plants kept in a cool position.

The soil for cacti is not especially abundant in nutrients owing to its high sand content, and cacti in flower pots have only a small quantity of soil available as a nutrient source. Hence, it is quite reasonable to manure them on occasions with a special flower manure which contains relatively little nitrogen but larger proportions of phosphorous and potassium. Such mixed fertilisers are produced nowadays by all large companies. The usual mixed fertilisers for the garden and horticulture are unsuitable for cacti owing to their high nitrogen content. The most favourable is a nitrogen : phosphorous : potassium ratio of 5 : 16 : 38. Every 10—14 days a 0.1% solution with this fertiliser should be prepared in the watering water, naturally only during the growth and flowering period, never during the resting period or after repotting.

Repotting is carried out when the resting period has ended. The starting of new growth is recognised by the fresh green colour at the tip of the cactus plant. In the majority of cases this will occur in spring. Cacti which flower in spring are transplanted only after they have finished flowering. Larger plants are best kept 2—3 years in the same pot; smaller cacti which are usually obtained in very small pots should be transplanted every year. The plant is carefully removed from the pot in order to observe whether fresh soil and a larger pot are necessary; the root ball is carefully moistened: the pot is turned upside down and knocked carefully by its upper edge against the table edge, so that the root is readily separated from the pot wall. Smaller plants are wrapped into thin paper, larger plants are enveloped into a soft cloth, so that no soil will settle between the spines.

If only a few bright and healthy root strands are observed outside the root ball then the plant is returned to the same pot and firmly replaced with light pressure. If a matted root tangle is found, then a larger pot is taken; its draining hole is covered with a piece of crock and a thin layer of coarse sand — in the case of larger pots, fine gravel — is scattered on top of it. After that, sufficient cactus soil is placed into the pot so that the root ball which is placed on top of it will not quite reach the upper edge of the pot. The remaining space up to the pot edge is filled with soil which is settled by slight tapping of the pot against the table top; no cavities must remain. Some cactus lovers like to arrange their globular cacti together in groups in earthenware trays or boxes. In this case the bottom of the container is first covered with a layer of broken crocks and then it is filled with fresh soil up to ½—1 cm (.25 in) below the upper edge. The roots (or the root ball) of the plants are held down and pressed slightly with the covering soil. It is debatable whether the root ball should be loosened before transplanting with a wooden stick or left undisturbed. Generally speaking no plant likes to have its roots poked.

Watering is carried out sparingly in the first few days after transplanting (under no circumstances must fertilisers be used) and the plants are kept in half shade.

Propagation

This is not difficult. It is carried out by sowing and by using cuttings. Seeds of cacti should be bought only from reliable seedsmen, who in turn obtain them from recognised growers; only this way, is it possible to grow the cacti expected. If cuttings are used, then it is reasonable to expect, with certainty, that the daughter plants will be the same as the parent plants. Propagation by cuttings is to be preferred especially when it is attempted to breed and grow especially beautiful species or types. This method also ensures that the plants will flower much earlier.

Propagation from seeds is, however, highly enjoyable — it is an attractive hobby to observe how, between the yellowish green or reddish green cotyledons, there appear the spiny globular shapes or stems, which are also frequently deep green or of reddish colour and then to see how they soon afterwards develop their special characteristics.

The seeds are best sown in sowing trays, which should be kept as warm as possible; in the winter they may require bottom heat, which can perhaps be provided by a stand placed over a central heating radiator — but only if the radiator is placed directly under the window. The cacti require light for germination; in fact they require a great deal of light right from the start. It is best to wait until a warm season of the year for sowing and then the sowing trays are placed on window sills in the sunshine where they must be covered with a glass plate or with white tissue paper.

Sowing is carried out using a seedling soil which is not excessively screened. A well proven composition has two parts of well rotted beech leaf mould, one part of peat moss and one part of quartz sand.

The seeds are sown fairly closely together and then covered lightly with quartz sand or with broken brick. The seedling soil must be uniformly moistened; if it is necessary to water, then the small pots or trays are placed in lukewarm water and the soil is allowed to be saturated from the bottom. The temperature during the day must be at least 20—25°C (70—78°F). In the night the temperature may fall to approximately 15°C (60°F).

The containers are covered with a glass plate up to germination. The freshly sown seeds can be protected by watering with a 0.15% solution of Albisal solution against the fungi which prevent propagation.

The majority of cacti will germinate after 2—5 days, or earlier in warm sunshine; opuntias and phyllocactus need up to 6 weeks. The seedlings should be kept in the sunshine; however, attention must be paid so that the sun does not burn them and that the soil surface does not dry out because the roots are still small and they can find moisture only in the surface layers of the soil. Seedlings are pricked out when they are approximately 6 months old. They are then still quite tiny and they must not even be gripped with a pair of pincers. The pricking out is, therefore, somewhat tiresome precision work. However, it is not advisable to postpone it. Cacti thrive better when they are planted relatively closely together than when they are spaced widely apart; after the first pricking out they should not be separated from spine to spine any further apart than their thickness and on the second pricking out, half their diameter is a sufficient separating distance.

The seedlings do not require a resting period, which is absolutely necessary for grown up plants. The seedlings can be moderately watered also during the winter when they are to be kept in a warm place. These will be planted individually into small pots after 1—2 years. Propagation by cuttings is very simple in the case of some globular shaped cacti which produce a large number of offsets; these are cut off from the parent plant. The cut surface must be allowed to dry for a while (usually a couple of weeks); if freshly cut cuttings are planted immediately, then they are sure to rot. The cut surface of the cuttings is dusted with charcoal powder and allowed to dry. They will soon form new roots when planted into a mixture of half sand and half peat moss.

The above is especially applicable to cuttings taken from opuntias, cereus and other cacti which do not form offsets and from which pieces of stem are cut for propagation purposes. The narrowest possible point is selected for making a cut and the lower end of the cut piece is chamfered into a slightly conical shape in order to improve the formation of roots. The cuttings are then placed upright in a tray and allowed to stay for drying purposes in bright light and in a not excessively cool place. They are then placed individually into small pots which are filled up to three quarters with cactus soil; a layer of sand and charcoal is scattered on top of this soil. The cuttings are watered very sparingly (and, of course, not fertilised), they are frequently sprayed with water and provided with bottom heat as far as possible. Once they have filled their small pots with roots, they are carefully placed with an undisturbed root cluster into a larger pot.

In the case of epiphyllum a cutting of length 15—20 cm (6—8 in) is cut from the previous year's shoot. The lower end is sharpened to an extent of 2—3 cm (.75—1.125 in) after which the cut surface is thoroughly dried, in an upright position, for a couple of weeks. The cutting is then placed so deep into the sandy cactus soil that both lowermost areoles (spine pads) just touch the soil surface — the best roots are developed from these points.

Grafting

This is actually quite amusing work but which also requires some experience with cacti. Grafting can also be carried out when the roots of an especially beautiful item have suffered from a disease; this plant is strengthened on a healthy, well growing stock. Alternatively a seedling can be brought earlier to flowering if it is grafted on an already mature older stock which is matured to the flowering stage: the juices which are supplied by the stock will also make the scion capable of flowering. The appearance of a globular shaped cactus grafted on a tall, slender stem will look somewhat peculiar; however, grafting has quite a few advantages.

The best time for grafting is the summer months from May to August. At that time both the stock and the scion are growing strongly and they will join rapidly. Various species of cereus are eminently suitable as stock; the *Trichocereus schickendantzii* lends itself readily to grafting and the grafting of cereus species as well as of the globular shaped cacti is successful in the case of *T. macrogonus* (especially for *mammillaria*), *T. pachanoi*, *T. spachianus* and *C. peruvianus*. The *Zygocactus* are usually improved by grafting on *Pereskia*, whose growing period is also wintertime. Also *Echinocereus pectinatus* and its hybrids should be grafted (on *T. spachianus*). The cutting is made with a sharp knife of stainless steel at that position where the new shoot starts — this can be recognised by a somewhat brighter green colour. The shoot should not yet have an internal callus on the cutting position. The uppermost areoles of the stock are cut off so that no side shoots will emerge and the freshly cut scion is placed on the stock so that the vascular tissues, arranged in circular pattern, (which are observed in the middle of the cut surface) will come into contact. The stock and the scion will not always have the same diameter — nor is this absolutely necessary, as long as the vascular tissues are placed together. The scion is slightly pressed down on mounting and it is slightly rotated so that air bubbles are expelled. A soft rubber ring is then placed over the scion and pulled uniformly on both sides under the pot or fastened on the sides onto the spines of the stock.

If milky juice emerges from the cut surface of the scion (for example, in *mammillaria*), then this is not to be wiped off but the cut scion allowed to rest until the milky juice flow has somewhat abated.

The grafted plants must be allowed to stay in a warm place, in dry air. If it is observed that they have not grown together correctly, then they must be separated, fresh cuts made on both parts and then placed together again. If they grow together well, then the rubber bands can be removed after 4 days in the case of soft species, and in the case of harder species, after 8 to 10 days.

Even seedlings of a few weeks old can be successfully grafted; they need not be pressed on juicy stock surfaces. If a piece is cut off from a still young valuable plant for grafting and improving purposes then there is a danger that the large cut surface will collapse on drying and rot. A covering graft is made in order to prevent this happening; a cover which has been cut, for example, from an offset of *echinopsis* is placed on a still freshly cut surface. If the stock produces shoots later somewhere, then these side shoots are cut off. The cut surfaces must be clean and as small as possible. The peculiar 'crest' or 'cristate' forms cannot be propagated from seeds but only by grafting. These coxcomb shaped extensions of the plant body are not a sign of a disease but a puzzling form of growth which has not yet been explained by science and which we also observe as 'fasciation' in raspberry shoots, in the flower stock of *digitalis* or in the *compositae* and which can also be seen elsewhere in nature. Among the seeds from such fasciated plants there are always only very few which inherit this cristate form. These occur relatively frequently in cacti and they are greatly liked by collectors because of their unusual appearance. A coral type growth form *(forma monstrosa)* of some cereus species is also peculiar and as yet unexplained. These will form a mountain range shape instead of a column and this is the reason why they are known as 'rock cacti'.

Pests and diseases

Cacti become actually diseased or become infested with pests only if mistakes are made in their care. Cacti need an airy, light position and regular moisture, and like to be undisturbed (a cool and light position with sparing watering) in their resting period and correct nutrition (which also means that neither the soil nor the water must be rich in lime) like all other plants.

The fungus which attacks growing plants can cause a great deal of damage in very young plants. A sunny, well aired position — no stagnant moisture — prevents the growth of rot fungi. In case of emergency a treatment with Albisal can be used (see section propagation). The greatest enemies are the independent and cyst forming root borers (nematodes). They can be eliminated during the warm season by watering 3—4 times with a 0.1% Nemafoss solution or by immersion in the solution or by mixing of 1—2 g Nemafoss granules into the planting soil. Both agents will also act against the root mealy bug. The red spider mites (or red spiders) are treated with Kelthane spray 1—2 times in a year (detailed instructions on the package). Soft fleshed species of globular shaped cacti and mammillaria will, on occasions, be subject, in wintertime, to dry rot which, unfortunately, is usually recognised too late because it destroys the internal tissue, while the outside tissue remains healthy. This disease is also caused by a fungus which penetrates into the plant body through small injuries, for example at the root base; corky, brownish spots appear which dry up so that hollow cavities are formed. The diseased plant can perhaps be rescued by deeply cutting off the diseased parts if the dry rot also appears on the outside skin. No effective means of combatting this disease have yet been found. This disease can be prevented by arranging that the plants are also in the sun in the wintertime and attention must be paid so that any damage (also that caused by insects) is prevented.

Among the insects, the red spider mite is very dangerous because it destroys the epidermis especially of young shoots and causes brown or yellow spots to appear at the tips of the cacti; this insect will also cover the plant body with a whitish web under which it can multiply very rapidly. The red spider mites appear especially when the air is dry and they select bright green species such as *rebutia* or *Chamaecereus silvestrii*. They cannot withstand moisture at all well and hence cacti which are regularly sprayed are relatively safe against this insect. However, once they have arrived they will multiply very rapidly and they can ruin complete collections within a very short time. They can be effectively killed by spraying or brushing with contact poisons such as Deril, Basudin or with phosphorus preparations in the prescribed solution strength.

Mealy bugs and root mealy bugs are also very tiresome. They are 1—5 mm (0.025—0.125 in) long and coloured white by waxy segregations which are water repellent and which protect these insects against many spraying agents. Unless they occur in large numbers they can be picked up with a sharp wooden splinter (care must be taken not to injure the skin of the plant). In the case of heavy infestation it is useful to spray or brush with one of the more recent agents used against the blood bug; these agents dissolve the waxy coating. In any case cacti, which have a bluish waxy coating on their epidermis must not be treated with these agents.

The root mealy bugs are more unpleasant because they cannot be treated without removing the cacti from the ground and removing the soil from their roots. In this case brushing with contact poisons is also most effective. However, such a treatment cannot usually be carried out without injury to the roots; the cacti must not be watered for 3—4 days after repotting. If good care has previously been taken to ensure uniform moisture in the pots then the infestation is only slight.

Scale insects like to reside especially on certain opuntias and on cerei. The young insects, which are hardly 1 mm (0.025 in) long, are highly mobile when young and they stick themselves firmly on to the plant and form a 2 mm (0.05 in) diameter round yellowish grey scaly shield under which they place their eggs. If the cactus lover, with the best intention, now removes these little plates with a wood splinter, then he runs the risk that the eggs or freshly hatched young insects will fall out and spread over the whole plant. More effective than this search (in which it is not possible to find all the scale insects) is the spraying or brushing with a contact poison which must be repeated every 14 days, so that the young insects which creep out from the shielding plates will also be killed.

If you place your cactus collection in the manure bed boxes in the garden during the summer then you will find that slugs and snails will attack the plants. The slugs are best trapped by positioning halved and hollowed out raw potatoes on the ground into which the slugs (who will eat only at night) will retire towards the morning. The best means against snails is the spreading of poisoned bait. Sometimes earwigs will eat the flowers; they will creep into their hiding places towards morning and it is possible to catch them if pieces of coarse, slightly moistened sponge or paper balls are placed between the pots.

The yellowish or brownish spots of 'sunburn' are signs of a disease, mainly in young, tender tissues; if the whole plant becomes yellow, then in many cases this has been caused by excessive watering. If, however, this is not the case then the plants must be knocked out of their pots, the roots carefully examined and all diseased parts cut off. The cacti are then placed on sand and peat moss until the freshly cut surfaces have dried out; the plant is then treated as a cutting.

The roots are also frequently diseased if the plants turn red. Such cacti must be positioned in the shade, after the diseased parts have been removed but they must be kept warm; further treatment must be as for cuttings. The red colouring can also occur in completely healthy cacti, if they receive more sunlight than they are accustomed to or if warmth loving species have been kept in excessively cool surroundings. The red colouring will vanish when the plants are placed in conditions agreeable to them.

Corky growth will occur frequently at the base of the stem in plants which have been kept in excessively damp and dark positions or which have been placed too closely together in a tray. This can be readily cured by transplanting, repositioning and by better feeding.

Classification of cacti

It is absolutely necessary for amateur growers of cacti to have some idea about their classification, which means their division into genera and species.

The cacti form their own family of plants known as cactaceae. From the point of view of plant ecology, which is the study of the society and environment of plants, they are designated as 'succulents' and especially as 'stem succulents', ie. they have developed a fleshy stem and for this reason they belong to the group of xerophytes or plants capable of resisting drought. These plants live in dry areas and they have adapted themselves to live with shortage of water. There are also 'leaf succulents', for example, sedum and sempervivum species; these plants have thick fleshy leaves.

There are altogether a total of approximately 4,000 species of cacti, the majority of which are not suitable for indoor cultivation. New species are added to these every year. This is not only because the collectors of cacti are still discovering new plants in the deserts, wastelands or in the jungle and that botanical gardens or large growers are creating new species, it is also because the classification of the cacti is continuously being changed: the specialists of the scientific plant classification systems find time and again within the already long known species, some which are distinguished from their companions by some special feature in such a manner that they are assigned to a new species.

At present the cacti have a total of approximately 200 genera. To us, who are neither interested in collecting cacti nor in their scientific research, however, the differences in the features of species are of little account. Wherever it is necessary to have a readily available and clear view then it is useful, even today, to use the classification of Professor Karl Schumann originating from the year 1898, which classifies the cacti into 21 genera. Even from among these we can eliminate some genera, because they include cacti which are rare and difficult to grow.

The survey below shows the typical features of the 11 more important genera, classified according to Schumann, which are useful for the amateur grower of cacti:

In our description of individual species of cacti we will keep to the above classification; however, we will identify the plants below by their currently used conventional scientific names. Hence the reader will not lose sight of the general picture and will still be in a position to identify his plants accurately.

The first part of the scientific name always designates the genus and the second word designates the species.

1. *Pereskia*

2. *Opuntia*

3. *Rhipsalis*

4. Christmas cactus
   Zygocactus

5. *Epiphyllum*

6. *Echinocereus*

7. *Cereus*

8. *Cephalocereus*
   and *Pilosocereus*

9. *Echinocactus*

10. *Echinopsis*

Lobivia

Rebutia

Rebutia
(*Aylostera*)

11. *Mammillaria*

1. **Pereskia** Shrub-like or trailing plants, with abundant foliage. These plants require very humid air and hence they are not suitable for indoor cultivation. Some species are found useful as grafting stock for *zygocactus.*

2. **Opuntia** The stem parts are usually flat, but they can also be cylindrical or globular. The flat opuntia are usually large plants, they will flower quite late and require a great deal of room. They are grown less for their flowers than for their glochid clusters which are frequently of interesting colours. The stem opuntia with cylindrical segments are smaller, and flower early. The globular opuntia have compact growth, they remain small and have beautiful flowers.

3. **Rhipsalis** Decoratively divided stem. The segments are cylindrical sticks, polygonal or flattened, the majority without spines. Original dweller in the jungle trees in South America and on the West Indian Islands. Flowers profusely in winter, but less suitable for indoor culture.

4. **Zygocactus** Includes the Christmas Cactus. This plant has a number of flattened stem segments without spines. It grows on trees in Eastern Brazil. The shape ranges from prostrate to trailing plants, suitable for growing in hanging baskets, it is also grafted as small tree-like extensions on *Pereskia*. Beautiful flowers in winter!

5. **Epiphyllum (Phyllocactus)** Whole segments (up to 50 cm (20 in) long) are flat and leafy, slightly notched. Beautiful breeds flower in summer.

6. **Echinocereus** Prostrate, usually branched, with strong spines; soft body without internal corky part. Large group. Originates from Arizona, Texas, Mexico, from wastelands with well defined rain and drought periods. Has beautiful large bright flowers in summer which last a long time.

7. **Cereus** Grows upright, trailing, creeping, and rambling. Widespread in USA, Central and South America; many species have beautiful blue or white waxy cover. Usually only older plants flower.

8. **Cephalocereus** and **Pilosocereus** Original home in America, like the above genus. Slightly less spectacular flowers, which appear only on older plants; also the luxuriant white hairy growth appears in some species only later. Requires a great deal of sun, heat and protection against dust.

9. Echinocactus Large genus which incorporates the best loved cacti. Globular growth, beautiful, often very early flowers. Mexican species especially require a great deal of sun and warmth for development of flowers, therefore they are not willing to flower everywhere as readily as the South American species.

10. Echinopsis and its subgenus **Trichocereus** Globular, elongated with age. Has splendid colourful flowers, whose tubes are long, covered outside with scales or hairs. With its home in South America, this is one of the best loved indoor cacti, it flowers profusely and readily and is easy to cultivate. *Lobivia* and the dwarf cacti were formerly incorporated with *echinopsis*.

Lobivia Globular growth, with short tubular flowers. Its longitudinal ribs are interrupted as tubercles under each areole. These plants originate in mountainous regions mainly in Bolivia and they require a very cool temperature for wintering. Flowers with bright colours appear in profusion, even in very young plants.

Rebutia, dwarf cactus. Flat and globular, very small. Flowers with free standing funnels appear in profusion, almost at the base of the plant body, even in very young plants.

11. Mammillaria Globular shape, sometimes slightly elongated. Closely spaced spines or hair. Body not ribbed or polygonal as in the genera 5 to 9, but covered with tubercles and the spines or hair grow at the tips of these protuberances. The flowers emerge from the axils between the tubercles. The plant body remains small and it has beautiful flowers which are arranged in a circle and for this reason it is popular with amateur growers. amateur growers.

Opuntia

The home of these plants is the whole of North and South America. They like a great deal of sun and they need to be especially warm in the summer, whereas in the winter they prefer a cool, light and airy position. Among the approximately 300 species the flat padded *opuntia,* with the exception of the *Opuntia mycrodasys* and its closer relatives, grow very large and hence they frequently become too large for indoor cultivation. Some winter-hardy species are suitable for the rockery. Here, they need sandy, very porous ground. They are more sensitive to damp than to cold, and in autumn they must be specially protected against rain so that their shoots will mature before the winter. A light winter covering of loose sticks is intended to protect plants less against the frost than against the sun which causes premature growth.

Flat padded *opuntia:*
Opuntia aureispina Small plant, also globular, with beautiful golden and brown spines.
Opuntia basilaris Habitat: Southern Nevada, Northern Sonora (Mexico); 1,200 to 2,700 m (4,000—9,000 ft) above sea level. Requires a great deal of sun. Winters at 6—10°C (42—50°F).
Opuntia bergeriana Grows as a shrub. Beautiful yellow spines. Readily produces a profusion of large red flowers.
Opuntia leucotricha Vigorous grower, long flat pads with white, twisted spines up to 8 cm (3 in) long.
Opuntia microdasys Small plants, golden yellow glochids, very numerous, without spines. Yellow flowers 5 cm (2 in) large.
Opuntia microdasys var. albispina Has white, nonprickly glochids, especially suitable for indoor cultivation.
Opuntia monacantha Cultivated on sunny slopes. Flowers profusely in the open. Frost-free wintering. Plants which grow too large can be cut back.
Opuntia rafinesquei Branched shrub type growth, prostrate. Yellow flowers with red centre. For rockery, winter resistant.
Opuntia rhodantha Medium vigorous growth, profusely branched, majority of pads reddish. Carmine red flowers. Also suitable for rockery.
Opuntia scheerii Up to 1 m (3.3 ft) tall, branched shrub-like plant, lemon yellow spines, between which grows silky soft hair. Very beautiful!
Opuntia soehrensii Decorative, cluster forming.

Cylindrical opuntia While the flat padded *opuntia* frequently become too large for indoor cultivation before they begin to flower, the cylindrical *opuntia* with cylindrical or globular segments are not especially vigorous growers·

Opuntia basilaris

Opuntia monacantha

Opuntia verschaffeltii

Opuntia clavarioides, 'Nigger's hand' Brownish grey joints, branched, hand-like shape. Grows best as scion on erect opuntia. Requires a great deal of warmth in summer, cool, light position in winter.

Opuntia salmiana Grows as a shrub with cylindrical joints. Flowers readily and profusely. Beautiful flowers, red outside and yellow inside.

Opuntia spegazzinii Compact growth, white flowers.

Opuntia verschaffeltii Small plant, almost without spines, with orange flowers. Simple care required, very good flowering plant on sunny slopes in open. Winters at 6—10°C (42—50°F).

Globular Opuntia *Globular Opuntia* are dwarf plants. If early flowering is required then they are placed in a very warm and dry position in summer:

Opuntia diadematus This plant, of prostrate habit, grows in clusters and has papery brownish spines. Similar to *T. papyracanthus.*

Opuntia hypogaeus Very small vigorously growing dwarf species.

Opuntia papyracanthus 'Papery spine cactus'.

Slender stemmed cacti, Rhipsalis

Attractive plants flowering in winter, for growing in hanging baskets, but not very suitable for indoor cultivation because, as dwellers on jungle trees, they require relatively high air humidity. Not conveniently accommodated in greenhouses owing to the trailing form of growth. Keep in warm light places during the growing period. Protect against direct sunshine, water regularly. Immerse the pot into fertiliser solution every 10 days, spray with water, drain well. Rest period in summer, water sparingly, keep in half shade. Only the following are suitable for indoor cultivation:

Rhipsalis pachyptera The segments are leaf-shaped, with strong middle and lateral veins, notched, and frequently reddish on the edges. Yellow flowers with pink tip.

Rhipsalidopsis rosea Segments flat and polygonal. Pink flowers in March—April. Reliably flowering plant. Grows best when grafted on *Eriocereus jusbertii.*

Rhipsalidopsis gaertneri
'Easter cactus'

Nopalxochia phyllanthoides

Zygocactus or Christmas Cacti

Also a tree dweller. These plants require humus rich, highly porous soil, they require warmth in summer but must be protected against direct sunlight. Spray frequently with lukewarm water (however, well advanced buds must not become wet!). They must always stay in a warm room. The flower buds drop off when the air is too dry and if they have insufficient potassium and phosphorus. Tall plants grafted on *pereskia* require a support stick. Allow a couple of weeks resting time in half shade after the flowers have dropped, keep in a cool position and water sparingly. Even if the shoots have a 'matt' appearance at first, they must not be watered more generously. Transplant only every 3—4 years; the root ball must not be destroyed in transplanting. Beautiful cultivated types with different shades of pink varying to bright scarlet red have been grown for more than 100 years. The present name *Zygocactus* is not yet widely introduced.

Rhipsalidopsis gaertneri or 'Easter Cactus'. Cultivated indoors in windows. Very light soil. pH approximately 5. Grafted best on *Pereskia* or on *Selenicereus*.

Zygocactus truncatus The most frequently grown Christmas Cactus. Most beautiful varieties: 'Meteor', 'Vesuvius', 'Madame Andree'.

Epiphyllum

Like the *Zygocactus* these are also jungle tree dwellers. They have been made especially suitable for growing indoors (crossing with *Heliocereus speciosus* which grows on the ground); profusely and readily flowering plants with very few demands (everybody's cactus).

The best position is on the window sill. Protect against draughts and bright sun. Buds appear early in the spring at the start of the growing period. Flowers April—June, depending on the breed. Water regularly after the flowers have dropped and spray frequently, then gradually begin to water more sparingly, keep warm in summer and not excessively dry. Water less in autumn; so that the shoots will mature well. Keep in water at 8—10°C (48—50°F); best in a light and airy position (it will, however, stand a darker position); water only sufficiently until buds appear so that the root ball does not dry out. Repot or plant directly after flowering into rich, highly porous soil (mixture of sand, well rotted garden manure, leaf mould, clay but also garden soil). Flowering will suffer if it is not allowed to rest in winter! The flowers appear from the areoles in the notches at the edge of the segment. Each areole produces a flower only once; hence the shoots which are several years old, all of whose areoles have flowered, must be cut off if it is intended to produce beautifully formed, profusely flowering plants.

Nopalxochia phyllanthoides Cultivate in the window; not excessively sunny in summer, but warm in greenhouses etc., light soil, pH 5.

Epiphyllum hybridum Cultivate as Nopalxochia. This is the only species produced by breeding. Scentless red flowers only open during the day; yellow and white flowers which open also at night have a strong scent. There are a large number of beautifully flowering, readily cultivated types, especially among the more recently bred varieties.

Epiphyllum hybr. (Phyllocactus)

Prostrate Echinocereus

These are plants from deserts in Southern USA and Mexico. They like a warm, airy, very sunny position (protect against direct sunshine in spring) and highly porous soil with some lime. They flower in summer and are then generously watered and frequently fertilised. Older plants form offsets on the stem base and have a flat root system, they are best planted into large pot trays. In winter they must have a light, cool and dry position. They are not damaged by night frost, if they are in a resting condition. They grow vigorously and well and flower profusely. Propagated readily in June—July by cuttings. The very beautiful, large flowers are pink, red to dark purple red. They become profusely branched already whilst young, with slim joints up to 2.5 cm thick.

Echinocereus albatus A magnificent plant from Mexico for *echinocereus* collectors, best cultivated by grafting.

Echinocereus berlandieri Prostrate, with erect shoot tips, profusely branched. Shoots resting on the ground will root immediately. The funnel shaped flowers are bright red with a pink centre.

Echinocereus blanckii Erect plant, up to 15 cm (6 in) tall. Flowers dark purple. Highly suitable for indoor cultivation.

Echinocereus chlorophthalmus

Echinocereus fitchii

Echinocereus hempelli

Echinocereus papillosus

Echinocereus procumbens Reddish hue. Edge spines white with brownish tips. Flowers violet with bright centre.

Echinocereus purpureus

Echinocereus pectinatus var. rigidissimus Cultivate in grafted form.

Echinocereus salm-dyckianus Stems sprawling on the ground have yellowish, red tipped spines. Funnel shaped flowers, up to 10 cm (4 in) long, noticeably 'carrot red'. Popular and well proven for indoor cultivation.

Echinocereus scheerii Similar to the above, flowers pinkish red up to 12 cm (4.75 in) long. Both species produce offsets so profusely on the base of the stem that they are best planted into large trays.

Echinocereus schwarzii

Echinocereus stramineus Grows in compact, dwarf form with shoots 4—5 cm (1.6—2 in) thick. The spines are long, straw-coloured to white in colour and are pinkish red in the young plant. This plant is grown for its remarkably beautiful spines. The purple reddish flowers appear only rarely.

Echinocereus viereckii Grows in the same manner as the above species; however, it produces a profusion of large, bright purple flowers. The small stems are thick and branch only in older plants (they grow especially well when grafted).

Echinocereus albatus

Echinocereus chlorophthalmus

Echinocereus scherii

Echinocereus gentryi, Mexico

*Echinocereus pectinatus
var. rigidissimus*

Echinocereus fitchii

Echinocereus coccineus Short stems and offsets, up to 5 cm (2 in) thick. Spines 1—2 cm (½—1 in) long, yellowish with brownish tips. Flowers scarlet red.

Echinocereus delaetii Small stems 20—30 cm (8—12 in) tall, spines yellowish, accompanied by white hairs 6—10 cm (2.5—4 in) long. Similar to the 'Old man cactus' *(Cephalocereus senilis).* Flowers greenish brown on the outside, bluish red inside. Only suitable for cultivating under glass: this plant must be protected against dust if its hair is to remain shining and white.

Echinocereus fendleri Only 10—20 cm (4—8 in) tall, irregular growth. The flowers which are very large (up to 12 cm (5 in) diameter), are pale to deep carmine red. Can also be grown in rich garden soil mixed with sand, must be watered well in summer; in winter keep in the light and very dry (however, the body must not shrink).

Echinocereus gentryi Mexico.

Echinocereus knippelianus Globular stem, produces offsets vigorously, few spines (no spines in the young plant). Prone to infestation by the red spider mite, requires hardening and moist air, must be brushed or sprayed in case of emergency with one of the more recently produced phosphorus preparations. Suitable for window sills.

Echinocereus puichellus Almost globular, with 12—15 ribs and with short spines. Flowers white to pink. Only for cultivation under glass.

Echinocereus subinermis

Echinocereus is botanically related to *Wilcoxia.* The stems have thin shoots, covered with fine white bristly spines. Grows and flowers especially well when grafted on *Cereus:*

Wilcoxia poselgeri Beautiful reddish pink flowers with dark centres, opens in the afternoon.

28

Echinocereus hempelii

Echinocereus papillosus

Echinocereus purpureus

Echinocereus schwarzii

Echinocereus subinermis

Echinocereus viereckii

Cereus

In its natural habitat it forms columns, candelabra and bushes several metres tall, and it is in general a tall plant. A very large group with more than 50 genera, which originate from areas with widely varying climatic conditions and which hence require different care in cultivation. The majority of *Cereus* will flower only as older plants of about 1 metre (3.3 ft) tall; the *Aporocactus, Cleistocactus, Haageocereus, Heliocereus, Nyctocereus* and *Seticereus* will flower earlier. Cultivation approximately as for *Epiphyllum* but more moisture required. Blue or white spotted species develop their wax coating on the epidermis best in full sunshine and hence they should not be sprayed.

Cereus from deserts. Readily growing, beautiful. Water generously in summer. If kept dry in dry air in winter they are then also able to stand lower temperatures (not below 8°C/46°F). Require addition of clay to the cactus soil:

Cereus chalybaeus Stems covered with blue spots, black spines. Very profusely and early flowering nocturnal flowering plant.

Cereus forbesii Not very branched columns, with blue spots. Spines in young plants pale brownish red. Readily flowering. Flowers white inside, with greenish red edges outside, up to 25 cm (10 in) long.

Cereus jamacaru Rapidly growing, cultivated plants up to 4 m (13 ft) tall. With blue spots, yellow spines, white flowers open at night. Grows also as a monster cactus but will not flower in this form.

Cereus peruvianus Erect, profusely branched, very well growing plant. Spines up to 6 cm (2.4 in) long, brown, with yellow base, later black. Flowers up to 18 cm (7 in) long, reddish brown outside, white inside. Has also monstrous non-flowering form.

Cleistocactus smaragdiflorus

Corryocactus brachypetalus Slim shoots, branched, with very long spines. Orange yellow flowers. Unsuitable for amateur growers without a greenhouse.

Haageocereus australis Dark green, with numerous ribs, with remarkable spines.

Haageocereus versicolor Light green stem, spines russet to yellow. Flower up to 9 cm (3.5 in) long, white. Also a beautiful cristate form.

Stenocereus dumortieri 'Screw cactus'. Light green, hexagonal ribbed, frequently twisted stems with yellowish spines. White flowers only in older plants.

Borzicactus icosagonus (formerly known as *Seticereus aurivillus),* 'Golden pillar'. Densely spaced yellow spines; stems up to 5 cm (2 in) thick and up to 80 cm (32 in) long. Vermilion coloured flowers. Cultivation under glass recommended.

The *Cerei* below are grown less for their flowers than for their beautiful spines. They require low humus, sandy soil with some lime and clay and they must be watered carefully: in summer they should be watered sparingly in cooler weather, kept continuously dry in winter and not below 8ºC (48ºF):

Stenocereus marginatus 'Pearl necklace cactus'. 8 to 16 cm (3–6 in) thick stem. Areoles bluish white felt covered 'like pearls on a string'. Flowers cherry red, white inside. Keep warm.

Myrtillocactus geometrizans Profusely branched. Shoots have white spots in curved lines, few spines. Highly decorative. Numerous small flowers, fragrant (nightflowering).

Pachycereus pringlei Vigorous, erect, branches at base. Large white felty areoles and yellowish spines with black tips. Flowers greenish white up to 7 cm (2.75 in) long.

Stetsonia coryne Stem cylindrical or ribbed, up to 50 cm (20 in) tall, 9–10 cm (3.5–4 in) thick, pale green. Remarkable bright long spines. Hardly ever flowers in cultivation.

Mountain dweller. Grows trailing over rocks or winding upwards on rocks, also as a shrub with thin shoots. Not a demanding plant to cultivate. Requires rich, highly porous soil, sun and warmth in summer and a cool place in winter in dry air. Readily brought to flower. Flowers are beautiful, large and fragrant (nightflowering).

Aporocactus flagelliformis Cultivated on balconies; protect, as with all cacti, against rain. Light and cool wintering place; withstands some frost if kept dry.

Aporocactus flagriformis More vigorously growing plant than *A. flagelliformis.* Flowers larger, scarlet red with purple edge.

Monvillea haageana

Aporocactus flagelliformis

Chamaecereus silvestrii Readily cultivated, also as crowning scion grafted on cereus. Large number of small, red flowers, but only in a light, cool wintering position!

Cleistocactus areolatus Slim stems, net shaped field divisions. Red flowers.

Cleistocactus baumannii Erect or trailing, up to 1 m (3.3 ft) long slender shoots. Flowers readily. Large number of beautiful flowers, orange to fiery red.

Cleistocactus smaragdiflorus Greyish green stems. 2 cm (.75 in) thick, densely covered with spines. Flowers readily. Flowers of interesting shape, bright red with emerald green edge.

Cleistocactus strausii Erect stem, up to 6 cm (2.4 in) thick. Bristly spines, white, densely covering the whole stem. Readily cultivated. Profusely flowering, carmine flowers.

Selenicereus grandiflorus

Eriocereus bonplandii Shrub-like, vigorously growing. Requires support. Especially older plants flower profusely. Flowers up to 25 cm (10 in) long, white.

Eriocereus guelichii Profusely branched growth, climbing. Flowers large, white.

Eriocereus tortuosus Shrub-like vigorously growing plant. Requires support. Flowers white, readily brought to flowering.

Heliocereus cinnabarinus Polygonal stem, similar to that of *Phyllocactus*. Red flowers. Not sensitive in cool position.

Heliocereus speciosus Shrub-like, profusely branched. Requires support. Spines yellow to brownish. Flowers beautiful carmine red, large. In winter requires light, dry moderate warmth and in summer warmth and sunshine.

Monvillea haageana Shrub-like growth. Thin shoots, long, with bluish spots. Profusely flowering. White flowers up to 15 cm (6 in) long, open at night.

Nyctocereus serpentinus 'Snake cactus'. Long shoots, only 2—3 cm (.75—1.2 in) thick. Requires supports in order to grow along them in twisted form. The uppermost shoot flowers profusely and readily. Flowers up to 25 cm (10 in) long, white, fragrant, open only at night.

Selenicereus grandiflorus 'Queen of the night'. Nightflowering trailing cereus. Flowers up to 30 cm (12 in) long, white, strong vanilla-like perfume. Open only for one night. Thrives best in the greenhouse.

The following are better suited for indoor cultivation:

Selenicereus macdonaldiæ Vigorous growth, very large flowers, up to 35 cm (14 in) long.

Selenicereus pteranthus syn. S. nycticalus 'Princess of the night'. Very beautiful flowers, however, without fragrance, shoots up to 3 cm (1.2 in) thick, with many aerial roots. Flowers up to 30 cm (12 in) long, white with brownish red cover.

Other beautiful *Selenicereus* plants:

Selenicereus boeckmannii Good growing plant. Shoots light green. Few branches.

Selenicereus hamatus Has very large flowers, robust. Suitable as stock for Christmas Cactus.

Selenicereus jalapaensis Very tall, readily flowering.

Selenicereus nelsonii Thin shoots, good grower.

All *Selenicereus* are nightflowering plants with white flowers and they are jungle plants. They grow partly on trees or climb upwards from the ground. They are not suitable for indoor cultivation because they require a high degree of humidity in the air and the majority of them grow too large. They are suitable for the greenhouse as climbing and trailing plants. They require humus-rich soil; in summer half shade, and always protection against the midday sun. These plants include, among others: *Acanthocereus, Dendrocereus, Hylocereus, Strophocactus, Wilmattea.*

Cephalocereus and Pilosocereus

The majority of these plants are covered from early age (but some only as older plants), with white, woolly hair. They are somewhat sensitive to grow and they must be protected against draught and dust. In summer they require humid air and in winter a temperature of not less than 15°C (60°F); hence they are best grown in the greenhouse. On indoor cultivation they should be placed in a small glass box. They are extremely sensitive to moisture in the soil; in winter, and in all cooler weather, they must be kept quite dry.

Cephalocereus palmeri Eight-ribbed stem, with beautiful blue spots, densely covered with long white hair. Reddish flowers.

Cephalocereus palmeri var. sartorianus Stems covered with white, silky hair, which form a thick mop especially at the top.

Cephalocereus senilis 'Old man cactus'. 3 to 4 year old seedlings in breeding. Highly sensitive to moisture in the soil.

Espostoa lanata Densely ribbed stem, completely covered in long white hair. Especially beautiful! White flowers, red outside.

Espostoa melanostele Multi-ribbed stem covered by white woolly hair, looking as though packed in cotton wool; yellow spines.

Espostoa sericata As *E. Lanata*. Especially the tip of the stem covered with dense yellowish white hair resembling a cap.

Oreocereus celsianus Short stems, 8—10 cm (3—4 in) thick. Even as a young plant covered with dense hair, with 5 cm (2 in) long white curls. Insensitive species, can be wintered in a very cool place.

Oreocereus trollii Multi-ribbed stems, densely enveloped with white hair, from which reddish brown or golden yellow spines project outwards.

Cephalocereus senilis (3 and 4 year old seedlings)

Echinocactus

This is a large group which includes about 40 cultivated genera. In general these cacti, which are the most popular after the *mammillaria,* require a warm, sunny position and soil with as low as possible lime content. The details of the handling are different for each genus, depending on their origin.

The species which are at home in South America are especially suitable for indoor cultivation. They like warmth and on warm sunny days they like continuous light half shade (the usual net curtains are adequate). They must be slowly accustomed to the sun in the spring. Water generously in summer and sparingly in winter in a cool position (about 10°C/50°F). The soil must be sandy and not too rich.

Echinocactus grusonii An impressive plant which every amateur gardener would like to have in his collection.

Ferocactus echidne A very readily flowering species.

Hamatocactus setispinus If you have two such plants then the flowers can be cross-pollinated. Especially beautiful fruits will appear the following winter.

Gymnocalycium andreae, baldianum and **ourselianum** Should be kept warm, but requires some shade. In these conditions they are especially readily flowering plants with large flowers in many beautiful, especially whitish, colour shades.

Gymnocalycium bruchii Very small (2 cm/.75 in), frequently forms colonies. Spines white, close to the body. They flower even as young small plants, white with pink mid-stripes, February—March.

Gymnocalycium denudatum 'Spider cactus', deep green, thin spines, usually spreading (more rarely close to body), somewhat twisted. Flowers 6 cm (2.4 in) large, white, also reddish. Readily flowering plant, which requires protection in spring against sun.

Gymnocalycium gibbosum Semi-globular, later elongated. Very beautiful spines. Long lasting white flowers.

Gymnocalycium mihanovichii var. stenogonum

Gymnocalycium monvillei Broad, globular, with tubercular ribs. Spines yellow, reddish bases, curved. Flowers up to 8 cm (3 in) long, white to delicate pink. Very beautiful, readily flowering species!

Gymnocalycium multiflorum Broad globular, deep green with bald top. Flat spines, yellow, outwards spreading. Numerous pink-white flowers near plant top.

Gymnocalycium platense Globular, greyish green, white spines reddish at the base. Not a demanding plant, flowers readily even as a young plant. White flowers, open only in full sunshine.

Echinocactus grusonii

Ferocactus echidne

Gymnocalycium andreae

Gymnocalycium baldianum and ourselianum

Gymnocalycium quehlianum Globular-flattened, bluish green with short, brownish spines. Can be relied upon to produce long lasting white flowers with red base.

The more sensitive species such as the beautiful *Homalocephala texensis,* which is deep green with strong reddish spines and with silky pinkish-yellow velvety flowers, will prosper indoors only if they are grafted on *cereus*. The *Echinocactus* are best propagated from seeds, because the majority of them do not readily form offsets. However, it is possible to promote the formation of offsets if they are 'beheaded' ie. their top is cut off.

Frailea cataphracta 'Moon cactus'. Flat globular shapes up to 4 cm (1.5 in) diameter, with tubercular ribs. Crescent shaped purple spots under areoles. Yellow flowers with pink base.

Frailea pumila Dwarf plant, only 2 cm (.75 in) diameter, broad globular; tubercular ribs. The flowers are yellow and open only in the afternoons in full sunshine.

Notocactus apricus

Notocactus concinnus Flat globular shape, small, shiny green. Vigorously growing and profusely flowering plant. Large flowers (7 cm/2.75 in), shiny yellow, red outside in February. Protect against midday sun!

Notocactus graessnerii Flat globular, can hardly be recognised under the tangle of golden yellow needle shaped spines. Flowers emerald green, small, long flowering. Readily flowering and beautiful for indoor cultivation.

Notocactus haselbergii Flowers usually very early in the year in the collection.

Notocactus leninghausii Light green broad stem. Top inclines towards the light, white woolly hair. Fine covering of thin, yellowish bristly spines. Bright yellow flowers, long flowering.

Gymnocalycium baldianum

*Gymnocalycium mihanovichii
var. stenogonum*

Hamatocactus setispinus

Notocactus apricus

Notocactus haselbergii

Parodia chrysacanthion

Parodia saint-pieana

Parodia sanguiniflora

Notocactus mammulosus Small, globular. Ribs divided into tubercles. Spines yellow with brown tips. Flowers yellow with red centre.

Notocactus ottonis Flat globular, small, with reddish brown and yellow spines. Reliable flowering plant. Flowers shiny yellow with red centres, lasting 3—4 days. Protect in summer against direct sunshine!

Notocactus scopa Globular, somewhat elongated, almost completely covered with short, white spines. Numerous flowers close to the plant top, deep yellow with red centre. Popular as cristate form grafted on *cereus*.

Notocactus tabularis Semi-globular, flattened top, bluish green. Dense white and partly brownish red sharp tipped spines. Flowers even as young plant, 6 cm (2.5 in) large, yellow with carmine red tubes and red centres. Readily cultivated, readily flowering!

Parodia are often cultivated in special collections because of their beautiful flowers and spines. They flower frequently even as small plants.

Parodia aureispina Small with golden yellow spines, ribs divided into tubercles. Golden yellow flowers. Readily flowering!

Parodia chrysacanthion

Parodia maassii Elongated globular, vivid green colouring, with woolly top and strong yellow spines. Flowers 3—5 cm (1.2—2 in), copper red.

Parodia microsperma Small stature, globular, ribs divided into tubercles. Flowers readily and profusely, even as a young plant. Flowers golden yellow to orange.

Parodia saint-pieana This plant can claim the record for continuous flowering.

Parodia sanguiniflora The most beautifully flowering plant of the genus.

Thelocactus bicolor Globular to cylindrical. Multi-coloured spines. Large purplish-pink flowers, dark inside.

Astrophytum capricorne

*Astrophytum myriostigma
var. columnare*

Astrophytum

These are *Echinocactus* whose home is Mexico. In summer they require a great deal of warmth and sunshine, and also in the winter a very light, dry position at about 8°C (48°F). They must be accustomed gradually to sunshine in the spring (protect against the midday sun!). The soil must contain no humus: water carefully and do not use fertiliser. Growing from seed is very interesting and rewarding.

Astrophytum asterias 'Sea urchin cactus'. Flat globular shape with eight flat ribs, on which domed, light grey areoles are situated. No spines. The flower appears from the top; it is large, yellow with a red centre.

Astrophytum capricorne Globular, vivid green with white spots. Long spines, curved like horns. Fragrant flowers, yellow with red centre. Different forms are cultivated.

Astrophytum myriostigma var. columnare 'Bishops Mitre'. Tall, globular, with five ribs. Covered with small white hairy tufts, no spines. The shiny, yellow flowers appear at the top.

Astrophytum niveum Globular with eight ribs. Covered all over with white spots, with up to 7 cm (2.75 in) long bristly spines. Flowers golden yellow with red base.

Astrophytum ornatum Body with white spots forming stripes. Spines golden yellow, becoming darker later. Flowers large, 7—9 cm (2.75—3.5 in), shiny yellow.

Astrophytum senile Initially globular, later a short stem. Profuse white woolly hair at the top. Spines like soft bristles, up to 10 cm (4 in) long, cover the whole body like a loose netting. The large, brilliant yellow flowers have a red throat.

Echinopsis

These were introduced into this country at the beginning of the nineteenth century. At present only bred species are cultivated and not wild forms. Highly suitable for indoor cultivation. They require sandy but rich soil and occasional fertilising; however, excessive nitrogen leads to profuse formation of offsets at the expense of flowers (the same will happen at too warm a wintering temperature). In spring the plants must be gradually accustomed to more sunshine, and in summer they must be protected against direct sun. They then require a great deal of fresh air (if possible, place in the open) and generous watering. In winter they require a cool position (down to 10°C/50°F). The funnel shaped flowers which first open in the evening appear from June onwards; they can be pollinated by insects and will produce seeds.

Echinopsis aurea Globular, vigorously growing, without offsets. Flowers reliably. Flowers golden yellow, also other colour variants.

Echinopsis (Trichocereus) bridgesii Erect, only slightly branched at the base. Blue spots, deep yellow spines. White flowers.

Echinopsis (Trichocereus) candicans Erect, produces offsets at the base. Shiny green with long golden yellow spines. Areoles with white woolly felt. Large fragrant white flowers.

Echinopsis (Trichocereus) chiloensis Vigorously growing stem, up to 70 cm (28 in) tall. Light matt green with honey coloured spines, white flowers. Suitable only for the greenhouse.

Echinopsis eyriesii Deep green, globular, with marked ribs. Brownish spines. The large white flowers will last for 24 hours. Wild variety!

Echinopsis (Trichocereus) huascha Light green, 4—6 cm (1.5—2.5 in) thick. Spines yellow to brownish. Yellow flowers (there is also a hybrid with red flowers).

Echinopsis kermesina Globular-flattened, small plant, with very large crimson flowers. Readily grown from seed.

Echinopsis leucantha Globular with somewhat sunken, woolly felt covered top. Spines brown with dark tips. White flowers, 15—17 cm (6—7 in) long, with the fragrance of violets.

Echinopsis leucomalla Stem plant. Completely covered with very dense, short white spines. Bright yellow flowers.

Echinopsis macrogonus Vigorously growing, bluish green stem. Short brown spines. Yellowish white flowers. Good grafting stock.

Echinopsis obrepanda Globular, slightly flattened. Spines dark brown, curved, and very sharp and prickly. Flowers up to 20 cm (8 in) large, green outside, white to pinkish-red inside.

Echinopsis spec.

Lobivia type

Lobivia from Bolivia

Lobivia famatimensis   *Lobivia jajoiana*

Echinopsis oxygona Lobed, greyish green plant. Grey spines with black tips. Flower large, 20 cm (8 in) long, pink outside, white inside. Keep dry in winter!

Echinopsis turbinata (E. gemmata) Globular, but also a stem plant. Spines deep brown to black. Flowers 15—17 cm (6—7 in) bluish green on the outside, white inside, jasmine fragrance. Large plants have 15—20 flowers. Wild variety!

Echinopsis spec. From the province Salta (Argentina).

Echinopsis (Acanthocalycium) violaceum Globular, matt green. Needle shaped, slightly curved, yellowish brown spines. Flowers bright purple-pink. Grows and flowers readily! Withstands full sunlight without shading. Does not form offsets; can be propagated only by seed.

Lobivia species are good flowering plants, which can be readily cultivated throughout the summer on sunny slopes when protected against rain.

Lobivia backebergii Globular, light green with golden brown spines. Vigorously growing plant. Flowers bright carmine.

Lobivia chrysantha Somewhat flat globular shape, with long turnip-like root. (Plant in deep narrow pots). Flower up to 7 cm (2.75 in) large, yellow with purple base.

Lobivia cinnabarina Globular, up to 15 cm (6 in) diameter. Shiny green, with light brown spines. Flowers scarlet red with darker anthers.

Lobivia famatimensis var. cristata Flowering cristate form, the pride of the collector.

Lobivia hertrichiana Globular, fresh bright green, yellow spines. Red flowers, blooming profusely throughout the summer.

Lobivia (jajoiana) = o haageana

Lobivia mistiensis

Lobivia rubescens

Lobivia, a new species from La Paz

Lobivia tiegeliana

Lobivia jajoiana Place in the open and protect against rain and keep in a cold place during the winter (about 6–10°C/42–50°F).

Lobivia haageana

Lobivia mistiensis

Lobivia pentlandii Columnar, deep green. Large number of varieties with different form and flower colours. Flowers usually orange to carmine.

Lobivia rubescens Globular, somewhat elongated. Especially beautiful spines (very long, blackish red) and flowers (buttercup yellow with carmine throats).

Lobivia sublimiflora Columnar, decorative, transparent spines, arranged as combs. Large flowers, irridescent carmine red with purple background.

Lobivia tiegeliana

Lobivia walterspielii Globular. Ribs split into tubercles. Profusely flowering, carmine red.

Lobivia A new species from La Paz.

Rebutia

Profusely and readily flowering globular dwarf cacti with beautiful and glowing colours. Especially suitable for indoor cultivation. Care: see *echinopsis.*

Rebutia aureiflora Globular, with reddish tinge, forms offsets. Flowers gold to buttercup yellow.

Rebutia deminuta Short columnar stems, forms offsets in profusion. Plentiful cherry red flowers.

Rebutia euanthema v. oculata Small columns with transparent spines. Flowers especially beautiful, graduating from inside to outside from reddish, orange, carmine red with dark deep carmine red coloured stamens.

Rebutia haagei Somewhat elongated globular, bristly white, comb shaped spines. Flowers pale to deep salmon pink flame colour. Beautiful, reliably flowering species.

Rebutia heliosa

Rebutia krainziana Flat globular, forms offsets. Beautiful light coloured spines. Flowers glowing deep red.

Rebutia kruegeri

Rebutia minuscula Fresh green, thinly placed bristly spines. Red flowers appear reliably and in profusion.

Rebutia pseudodeminuta As *A. deminuta.* The orange-red flowers are frequently larger than the plant body and appear profusely.

Rebutia senilis Light green, covered with long white bristles. Red flowers.

Rebutia spegazziniana Columnar, short spines close to body. Beautiful red flowers.

Rebutia violaciflora Globular, golden brown spines, beautiful, purplish-pink flowers.

Rebutia wessneriana Globular, up to 8 cm (3 in) diameter. Transparent spines up to 2 cm (.75 in) long. Large (5 cm/2 in), bright blood red flowers.

Rebutia heliosa

Rebutia kruegeri

Mammillaria

A genus with a large number of species, whose home is exclusively Mexico and the adjacent countries. Globular and cylindrical shapes with spines of a wide variety of shapes and colours. Readily flowering even as young plants. The flowers, of beautiful colours, are usually arranged in circles around the top of the plant body and they readily form coral red fruit. Highly suitable for indoor cultivation. The *mammillaria* like a great deal of light, protected against direct sunshine in spring. Water generously in warm summer weather. Keep dry in winter at 8—10ºC (48—50ºF). Some sand should be added to the soil. Older plants produce offsets profusely and they are best kept in wide trays.

Mammillaria albilanata The fruits are also often very beautiful and will keep for some months.

Mammillaria bocasana Globular, later elongated with dense white bristles between tubercles. White spines, yellowish to brownish red. Flowers: early in spring, light red with deeper mid-stripes.

Mammillaria calacantha Globular, slightly elongated. Spines partly close to the body, partly outwards spreading. Flowers carmine red. Vigorously growing, readily grown from seed.

Mammillaria caput-medusae 'Medusa's Head cactus'. Broad globular, greyish-green with grey woolly felt and reddish spines. The flowers are bell shaped, white with pink mid-stripes.

Mammillaria carnea

Mammillaria coronaria Globular. Spines deep red to brown, on small, short tubercles with transparent radial spines. The small, light carmine red flowers with deeper shaded mid-stripes are arranged in a circle.

Mammillaria albilanata

Mammillaria carnea

Mammillaria glochidiata

Mammillaria guelzowiana

Mammillaria mazatlanensis

Mammillaria geminispina syn. M. bicolor Thick columns, closely enveloped with white clusters of spines. Flowers light pink with carmine red stripes.
Mammillaria glochidiata Small flowers, areole forming, attractive species.
Mammillaria guelzowiana Show plant with large flowers, unfortunately somewhat temperamental. Recommended to experienced collectors with greenhouses.
Mammillaria hahniana Small globular, white spines. Small purple-red flowers.
Mammillaria mazatlanensis Also belongs in the greenhouse and is especially grateful for this.
Mammillaria nivosa Unremarkable flowers, however, this is more than compensated by the fruits.
Mammillaria plumosa Globular, small. Spines feather-shaped. Small white flowers. Beautiful, interesting and popular plant, sensitive to damp and must not be sprayed. Grows well when grafted on cylindrical *mammillaria*. Needs sandy soil, whose surface is covered with a thin layer of powdered charcoal.
Mammillaria pringlei Globular. Yellow spines, twisted over the length of body. Carmine flowers.
Mammillaria prolifera Small, globular. Forms a profusion of offsets which will fall off and take root. Spines white and yellow, also reddish brown. Flowers greenish yellow.
Mammillaria rhodantha Similar to *M. pringlei*. Many hybrids with different colours, also yellow spines. Fiery carmine red flowers.
Mammillaria sheldonii Whole clusters of these plants are a joy to the eye during the flowering time.
Mammillaria spinosissima Thick, columnar stem. Closely covered with outwards spreading bristly spines, which are usually yellow, but can also be of blood red colour. Flowers in rings, carmine red.
Mammillaria theresae This belongs to the newer breeds. An areole forming plant which is cultivated best when grafted and under glass. Very profusely flowering plant.
Mammillaria viereckii Globular, small, and completely covered with yellow and white spines. Cream coloured flowers with greenish throat appear readily and profusely. Soil with some clay added.
Mammillaria wiesingeri Globular with slender tubercles which carry glassy white, spread out radial and reddish brown central spines. The flowers are a beautiful pink with carmine red mid-stripe.
Mammillaria wildii Slender columnar stem; forms offsets profusely. With white and honey coloured spines. White flowers arranged in circles. Very reliable, readily cultivated flowering plant. Water generously in summer and protect against sun.

Mammillaria nivosa

Mammillaria sheldonii

Mammillaria yaquensis

Mammillaria theresae

Mammillaria zephyranthoides

Mammillaria zeilmanniana Small thick columns, up to 6 cm (2.4 in) tall, with white and reddish brown spines. Even very small plants will produce bright purple red flowers. It flowers profusely also in cristate form.

Mammillaria zephyranthoides As above, unfortunately sensitive to damp; however, a magnificent plant.

Pseudomammillaria decipiens Small, with slender tubercles about 1 cm (.375 in) long. Long, thin, brown or white spines with dark tip. The flowers are white and often appear as early as December. Reliably flowering plant.

Dolichothele baumii Small, globular, cluster forming. Forms long turnip-like roots, so plant into deep narrow pots!

Dolichothele longimamma Areole forming, with yellowish spines on long, thick tubercles. Large yellow flowers. Requires half shade. Readily infested by red spider mite.

Mammillaria yaquensis Interesting plant: it will readily attach itself by its hooked spines to the clothes of the collector. It likes to be as close as possible to the glass.

Various species

Ariocarpus fissuratus Very difficult to detect in its natural surroundings owing to its camouflage. Ariocarpus originate from Mexico; they flower in autumn and they must be cultivated under glass.

Borzicactus samaipatanus Beautiful, prostrate, shrub-like species, flowers in a sunny position in the open and under glass.

Leuchtenbergia principis An unusual plant which is more like an Agave, whose long tubercles carry straw coloured, long and curved "spines". Its home is Mexico and it requires a great deal of sun and warmth in the summer.

Matucana (Borzicactus) icosagona A very beautiful plant with golden yellow spines, which flowers already when its size is 30 cm (12 in). Home: Ecuador and Peru.

Ariocarpus fissuratus

Borzicactus samaipatanus

Leuchtenbergia principis

Matucana (Borzicactus) icosagona

Index